Perched in the Soul:
Poems of a Birder

Judith Davis

BookLeaf Publishing

India | USA | UK

Presentation by *BookLeaf Publishing*

Web: www.bookleafpub.com

E-mail: info@bookleafpub.com

ISBN: 9789360941536

First edition 2024

*To my dearest loved ones, Anne and Jamie,
who encourage my birding and writing
poetry and perch their love in my soul.*

ACKNOWLEDGEMENT

Friends in the Cape Cod Bird Club, the Transylvania County Bird Club in North Carolina, and professors and colleagues in the Great Smokies Writing Program of The University of North Carolina in Asheville have enhanced my birding and writing poetry. A few of these poems have been published in the following journals: "Winter Visitor" in "The North Carolina Bards Poetry Anthology" 2022,
"A Tribute to Robert Frost" in "The North Carolina Bards Poetry Anthology" 2023, "Kanasgowa" and "Great Chieftain among the Woodpecker Tribes" in "Chiaroscuro, Brevard College Literary and Arts Journal" 2023, "Buzzy Spring Visitors" and "Spring Migration at our Pond" in "Chiaroscuro, Brevard College Literary and Arts Journal" 2024

PREFACE

When I heard and saw a beautiful Red-winged Blackbird in a wetland on Block Island off the coast of Rhode Island in 1995, I became a birder. When I retired from my career as a college professor and Episcopal priest, I began writing poetry about birds and did more paintings and photographs of birds. Birds have become my feathered friends and they have brought me much joy as I image them perching in my soul. I offer these poems as a reflection of my love for birds and birding in the hope that your own life may be lifted up to these feathered friends.

Advent

Advent

Crisp, cool mornings are warmed by the sun.
Eastern Bluebirds sit on the powerline,
Ring-necked Ducks gather at Carolina Lake,
Hooded Mergansers abound at our favorite
pond.
Blue Ridge Mountains show faint traces of
snow.
Leaves swirl around winter trees.
Christmas lights appear around town.
The Advent wreath is set up at Church.
Sarum Blue is the color for Advent and
We hear comforting words from Isaiah:
"The wolf will lie down with the lamb,
They will beat their swords into plowshares,
And a little child shall lead them."
Slow down, savor these days.
Listen to the birds. Be renewed.

Ash Wednesday

Ash Wednesday

Sunlight flowed softly blue through fog this
morning and two doe,
young female deer, darted into the yard as I
drove by.
Crows called back and forth, a White-breasted
Nuthatch,
two Carolina Chickadees, and four Tufted
Titmice ate our seed.
Four White Squirrels played on the bank of the
road, while
American Robins foraged on the lawn,
Gray clouds moved into the blue sky, but
Daffodils painted the lawns white, yellow, and
green.
A Turkey Vulture soared in the distance on this
Ash Wednesday as
I distributed ashes, reminding us of our fleeting
lives:
"Remember that you are dust," Dust of the earth
as well as stardust.

Autumn's Last Stand

Autumn's Last Stand

The row of Bradford Pear trees on the Asheville
highway seems like
Autumn's last stand since everything else has
turned brown.
Late fall air is crisp and cool and the brown
leaves in our driveway
crunch under my feet when I walk to the
mailbox.
Carolina Chickadees, Dark-eyed Juncos, Eastern
Towhees, and Tufted Titmice
remain feeding on our deck while summer birds
have migrated south.
White-breasted Nuthatches and Red-bellied
Woodpeckers
hang around with a murder of Crows.
I grab my old blue jacket from the coat tree in
the garage
and make sure my gloves are in the pockets.
The Blue Ridge Parkway will close soon, but the
blue silhouetted mountains
rise above in the distance, the sunset lighting
them up.

I love the view--the pink sky with blue
mountains and my birds.
I don my gloves and go in search of Autumn's
birds.

Beach Birds

Beach Birds

Brown Pelicans flew in formation low over the ocean.
Royal Terns darted quickly back and forth over the waves.
Busy, hurrying Sanderlings ran around the surf looking for supper.
Great Black-backed Gull caught a Spider Crab.
My heart soared with joy to feel the cool water on my bare feet
And the gentle breeze in my hair after so long.
Brown Pelicans and Laughing Gulls, my friends.
The ocean, my happy place
The warm sun and sand, my cheerleaders,
The sound of waves gulls, and terns, my choir.
The rhythm of the waves, my muse.
The beach, my happy home.

Christmas Bird Count

Christmas Bird Count

Some birds seemed to hide in the cool, damp
morning.
Finally, Eastern Bluebirds, American
Goldfinches, and Song Sparrows greeted us as
we counted them for Audubon's annual
"Christmas Bird Count."
A lovely Hermit Thrush posed for us and
followed us for a time.
A White-breasted Nuthatch did upside-down
antics.
Lots of Black Vultures soared overhead.
A White-crowned Sparrow, some Eastern
Bluebirds, and three Dark-eyed Juncos greeted
us at Fred's Farm.
A Cooper's Hawk guided us out.
Two Snow Geese grazed with a hundred Canada
Geese.
A lone Great Egret flew with twenty Great Blue
Herons.

Early Winter on our Mountain

Early Winter on our Mountain

Trees are bare now on our mountain.
Chickadees and Titmice are grateful for seeds.
Downy is glad for suet.
Gray squirrels chase each other in our woods.
Winter air is cool and brisk and I drink hot
coffee again.
Two large crows arrive on our deck.
Sam cat watches them.
The quiet is lovely.
Sunlight dances on dewy leaves of mountain
laurel,
and I expect, on our lake.
I love the peaceful morning.
Great Blue Herons seemed ethereal on the foggy
pond.
Snow Geese were camouflaged among the
Canada Geese.
White-crowned Sparrow posed on the fence.
Carolina Wren sang to me.

Fall Migration

Fall Migration

Gorgeous Monarch Butterfly floated nearby on
the golf course.
Red-tailed Hawk squawked overhead while
American Goldfinches sang.
Wilson's Warbler flew out of the wetland at the
college and landed nearby,
becoming a first-of-the-year sighting for my
"eBird" list.
Ruby-throated Hummingbird rested on a small,
bare branch of a Maple.
Downy Woodpecker perched on our suet feeder.
Northern Cardinals ate seeds on the deck.
Two White-breasted Nuthatches perched on the
suet.
I love fall migration!

Favorite Small Shorebirds

Favorite small shorebirds

My favorite small shorebird is a tiny Piping
Plover I first saw on Cape Cod.
Diminutive and lovely, the bird runs quickly
along the sand dunes seeking
food, its orange legs and bill catching the sun's
reflection.

Some beachgoers, known as "Summer People,"
complain when the nesting
grounds are roped off for the endangered Piping
Plovers and Least Terns.
Birders are rewarded when the chicks emerge
along the dunes in June.

Plover chicks, like cotton balls on tiny legs, hide
under their mother's wings.
Least Tern chicks are larger with long tails and
black bills with a touch of yellow.

Least Terns fly low over the water with quick,
deep wingbeats and shrill cries.
Piping Plovers run a few steps and pause, run
again and peck the sand for food.

I love early summer when I see the nesting area
of the dunes protected.
I rejoice when I see the tiny chicks which give
me hope for the world.

Full Moon Shines Brightly

Full Moon Shines Brightly

Full Moon shines brightly through the bedroom
window.
Stars dot the clear night sky. The night air is
cool.
A Barred Owl calls in the distant woods.
The night is quiet--no traffic to be heard.
I love our quiet mountain home, the clear, cold
night.
I love the stillness and peace.
I love the sunrise from this day, the woods
coming to life with
birds flocking to our feeders.
I drove to the pond to see the ducks, herons, and
mergansers.
A Red-tailed Hawk greeted me and a Turkey
Vulture flew by.
Kingfisher sang to me from the power line.
Buffleheads dove out of sight.
Great Blue Herons and Bald Eagles sit on their
nests now.
Fifty American Robins and two White Squirrels
made me smile.
Spring is coming. I can feel its hope for us after
the winter of our discontent.

Great Egret the Sentinel

Great Egret, the Sentinel

Great Egret, you stood sentinel along the shore
of the harbor at low tide—   making
a beautiful silhouette with the sun shining at
your feet.
You listened and watched for the quick
movement of the fish, your breakfast.
I sat in perfect stillness watching you fish on the
beautiful morning.
Sun danced on the glassy harbor and called to
both of us in a moment of peace.
How I will miss our quiet times of communion,
our times to be still and know   God's creation,
peace and quiet, as I sail from this harbor with
other birds than you over lakes and mountains to
a new home.
I will look for you as you and I migrate south,
and I will always give thanks to you and your
cousin the Snowy Egret with yellow feet.
We have loved this harbor of peace, our
anchorage, our spiritual home.

Hummer, Warbler, and Wasp

Hummer, Warbler, and Wasp

Ruby-throated Hummingbird found our new red
Tractor Supply feeder the first week in April at
our mountain home where he drank delicious
nectar.
Sporting a handsome ruby collar, like a
gentleman caller, he danced
from one red plastic flower to another.
A wasp joined him on the feeder sharing nectar
as if they were old pals from last fall.
Hummer and Wasp danced to an undetectable
rhythm nonplussed by each other.
Songbirds too, especially warblers, arrived on
that lovely April afternoon,
singing their buzzy songs to potential mates.
Hooded Warblers sang "zee-zee-zee-zoe-zee"
while Black-throated Greens
sang ascending "buzz, buzz, buzz, buzzzz"
notes.
Northern Parula dressed in blue-gray, green,
white, and yellow sang
"bz-bz-bz-zip" as if to say, "look how handsome
I am."

Spring in our mountains reminds me of words of
an old hymn:
"…God made their tiny wings."

A Tribute to Robert Frost

A tribute to Robert Frost

I know a place where Beech trees grow,
in the winter woods deep with snow,
a place where green moss clings to trees
while I watch a flock of Chickadees.

The woods are quiet, clear and cool,
where a painted turtle pops up from the pool,
and in the stillness of air and trees,
I hear the whispered flutter of Chickadees.

I love the quiet of the forest path,
I hear the voice of God at last,
a voice that comes in quiet calm
and warms my heart with loving balm.

I would stay in this deep and quiet place,
If only life would slow down a pace,
and I could build a tree house here
and love God's creatures who are near.

I must go home this New Year's Eve,
as I work and care and take my leave
of this sanctuary of time and place

with its lovely birds who sing with grace.

Next year will come in a few short hours
and I will explore birds in trees and bowers.
I will seek quiet and joy and peace
and not forget this day of ease.

Invitation to Birdwatching

Invitation to Birdwatching
Please accept this invitation to join me
birdwatching,
Not in my backyard, but out on trails and the
lake at the nature preserve.
Many of your feathered friends will join us for
our morning walk.
I issued invitations to them as well.

Spring suggests it might arrive anytime now.
I heard the peepers last evening.
Birds are already carrying nesting material.
I saw the elegant Great Blue Heron hurrying to
the rookery with a twig in its bill.

High overhead I saw the beautiful Bald Eagle
carrying a twig as well.
The Great Horned Owl has already accepted my
invitation.
Now she sits on her nest high in the bare tree
and it's just mid-February
She seems to be sitting on eggs and raises her
ear tufts so I see her.

Songbirds seem to be pairing up now like the
herons and owls and eagles have.
I saw a pair of Eastern Towhees on the ground.
Several Eastern Bluebirds sit on the power line.
Tiny Ruby-crowned Kinglets dart back and forth
in small trees.

Song Sparrows and Swamp Sparrows hop
around the boardwalks.
Virginia Rail calls in the marsh; that's rare for
February.
Migration is always a delightful surprise as I
dust off my binoculars.
Will you join me in Spring's delight?

Island Birds

Island Birds

A song I did not know came wafting from the
wetland on Block Island.
Looking into the marsh, I saw him perched on
the reeds, with brilliant red epaulets.
His name was Red-winged Blackbird, but I
didn't know the bird names then.
The Red-winged became my "spark" bird and
made me a birder.
I looked for birds on the islands of my life from
then on-- Bear Island, Bermuda, Block Island,
Cape Cod,
Cuttyhunk, Hispaniola, Hog Island, Star Island,
and Vancouver Island.
A King Rail called from the marsh on Bear
Island.
A Red-billed Tropicbird soared near me in
Bermuda.
A Ring-necked Pheasant visited me on Block
Island.
A Black-capped Chickadee ate seeds from my
hands on Cape Cod.
A Warbling Vireo sang to me on Cuttyhunk.

A Magnificent Frigatebird loomed large on
Hispaniola.
A Black Guillemot swam near me off Hog
Island.
A Spotted Sandpiper showed me her chicks on
Star Island.
A Rhinoceros Auklet teased me on Vancouver
Island.
A Red-winged Blackbird sang to me as I sang
"Morning has broken.
Blackbird has spoken like the first bird."

Kanasgowa

Kanasgowa [KAH-na-SKOE-wa]: Heron

My herons on Cape Cod, how I will miss you as
I move to the Carolina mountains,
Where the Cherokee named you Kanasgowa, the
Heron.
One autumn, almost a decade ago, we migrated
north to Cape Cod, and now we will migrate
south—you to the shores and salt marshes, and I,
to the mountain lakes.
I will look for you herons on the lakes as I long
to see you again.
You my favorite, majestic one, the Great Blue
Heron—
You, the diminutive Little Blue Heron—
You, the visiting Tri-colored Heron that I added
to my "life list."
You, the elusive one, the Green Heron with
several colors in the spring, yellow near your
eyes, green and maroon on your wings—
And you herons of dusk I watch flying to your
roosting trees.
We enjoyed the quiet of the salt marsh together
as you fished for supper.

You flew to your roost at dusk, and I counted
you for my "year list."
I will miss our peaceful, quiet times in the
evening by the marshes of   Cape Cod.
 I wish us blessings as we migrate to our new
homes.
You will migrate back to Cape Cod next spring,
and I will wait patiently for your return to our
mountain lakes, for you, Kanasgowa, will
always be in my heart.

Lord God Bird

Lord God Bird

John James Audubon named the bird "Chieftain Among the Woodpecker Tribe."
The Woodpecker was nicknamed the "Lord God Bird" because people cried out "Lord God, what a bird!" when they saw its incredible size and beauty.
Famous ornithologists saw it in the 1930s.
Audubon called the huge, two-foot long bird "graceful in the extreme."
The flame-red crest and huge ivory-colored bill marked the Ivory-billed Woodpecker.
The beautiful birds fed on beetle larvae in the American South's lowland swamp forests until logging destroyed their habitat.
Audubon and Peterson painted watercolors of the birds and taxidermists preserved the birds for history.
Declared officially extinct in 2021, the unique bird disappeared seemingly forever.
Rachel Carson warned us about losing these and other species, writing in Silent Spring that we had "silenced the re-birth of new life."

How we birders long to see the "Lord God
Bird," now gone from us and our children.
May we work to save our birds and our world so
the future will not be a Silent Spring.

Sherwood Forest Sonnet

Sherwood Forest Sonnet

Eastern Tiger Swallowtails flew by us
As we four played golf at Sherwood Forest.
Red-spotted purples joined us on the green
And flew over from the blooming pink Phlox.

I know that spring has found us once again
And warmed our old arthritic joints anew.
I loved playing golf today with my friends
And seeing warblers, blooms, and butterflies.

I wished I had binoculars with me
To see the buzzy warblers hiding near.
Migrating warblers were high in the trees.
I squinted to see them in the branches.

A wonderful day of golf and friendship
Made even more perfect with winged gifts.

Spring Migration

Spring Migration

Blue-winged Teal formed a chorus line in the
water.
Red-breasted Mergansers did synchronized
diving.
Great Blue Herons sat on nests at the rookery.

A single Bald Eagle flew across the pond.
Blue and white Tree Swallows skimmed the
pond for food.
Leaving one to tend the nest, Canada Geese
went for a swim.

A few Ruddy Ducks lingered on the pond this
winter.
A raft of Double-crested Cormorants stood
drying their wings.
Northern Mockingbirds and Northern Cardinals
perched in small trees.

Buzzy Warblers called in the trees and were too
evasive to be seen.
Song sparrows and Eastern Towhees sang their
songs.
I love Spring migration in our mountain home.

Winter Birds

Winter Birds

I sat by the fireplace on a cold winter afternoon
and watched the cold birds at our feeders and on
our deck.
Northern Cardinals and Carolina Chickadees
seemed nonplussed about the cold
while Dark-eyed Juncos happily ate birdseed
from the deck.

Enjoying a warm cup of coffee by the fire, I
wondered how the birds cope with winter.
A dozen American Goldfinches dressed in their
winter plumage happily ate the seed.
A few Pine Siskins joined them and seemed fine
about the cold.
Maybe I am the only one worried about the cold
today.

Two Dark-eyed Juncos came by for a snack.
The White-breasted Nuthatch enjoyed the suet
hanging from the roof.
A Red-bellied Woodpecker joined the Nuthatch
eating suet
and each of them seemed grateful for their treats.

A lovely Hermit Thrush flew in and landed on
the deck, catching a snack as well.
Two Mourning Doves joined the Hermit Thrush
in the late afternoon.
How delighted I am with these winter visitors!
What beauty and life they give to me each day!

Winter Day at the Pond

Winter Day at the Pond

My hands seemed frozen as I scoped out ducks
on the pond
in deep winter with a brisk wind on my face.
How I wanted to be warm at home sitting by the
fireplace,
But then I would have missed the winter ducks
today.

We birders go out in all kinds of weather looking
for our winter birds,
Especially ducks on the ponds, even when a thin
layer of ice makes
A skating rink for the Mallards and a landing
pad for Buffleheads.
I love seeing the great variety of winter ducks
even when my hands are cold.

Look, two Buffleheads have landed near a dozen
Hooded Mergansers.
I love the white patches on their heads and their
dark bodies as they swim along.
They seem to enjoy their winter swim while I
am freezing

And wishing I had hand warmers and a hot cup
of coffee.

Canvasbacks have joined the other ducks and a
dozen Canada Geese fly overhead.
Pied-billed Grebes and Common Mergansers
dive for food.
A Belted Kingfisher calls to them from the
powerline over the pond
and the beautiful Bald Eagle swoops over the
pond catching a fish.

Winter Visitor

Winter Visitor

"A Snowy Owl is at the Beach," birders reported
in the winter of 2014.
I grabbed my camera, binoculars and heavy coat
and drove to the beach.
Cars were parked near the marsh side and
birders were poised with their cameras.
Expecting the owl to be out on the marsh grass, I
was surprised to see it nearby.
My heart leapt on seeing the graceful, white
bundle with brilliant yellow eyes staring
at me, and becoming a "life bird" as it posed on
the snow-covered marsh grass.
My fingers froze on the camera's shutter in the
fifteen-degree, windy afternoon, but
my soul was warmed with delight on seeing the
incredibly beautiful bird.
What a memorable gift of joyful life on a very
cold February afternoon.
My image won a juried photography exhibit and
now graces my living room wall.
I smile every time I see it and remember that
remarkable day when
I fell in love with the Snowy Owl at first sight.

www.ingramcontent.com/pod-product-compliance
Lightning Source LLC
LaVergne TN
LVHW010939200726
843509LV00013B/2252